Jellyfish
Still Can't Swim

radiant star books
AN IMPRINT OF **bright sky press**

2365 Rice Blvd., Suite 202
Houston, Texas 77005

10   9   8   7   6   5   4   3   2   1

Library of Congress Cataloging-in-Publication Data

Parker, Marjorie Hodgson.
pages cm
ISBN 978-1-939055-13-2
1. Children—Prayers and devotions.
2. Animals—Religious aspects—Christianity—Juvenile literature. I. Title.

BV4870.P36 2013
242'.62—dc23   2013016029

Editorial Direction, Lucy Herring Chambers
Creative Direction, Ellen Peeples Cregan
Design, Marla Y. Garcia

Printed in Canada through Friesens

Jellyfish
Still Can't Swim

The Secrets of God's Creatures that
Make Them Good Teachers

Marjorie Hodgson Parker
Illustrated by Tim Davis

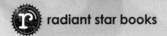 radiant star books

Solomon, who was the wisest of kings,
Noticed the habits of many small things.
In Proverbs, he spoke of the wise ways of creatures.
King Solomon thought even ants could be teachers!
Habits of creatures both great and small
Teach awesome lessons of God to us all.

TO MY READERS

I'm so happy that you are reading this book—you are the second or third generation to do so! I wrote the original book, *Jellyfish Can't Swim,* when my own children were small. This time, with new animal friends, I'm writing for my grandchildren. I've also included the first devotional that gave the book its name because, just as God's teachings still hold true (and they always will), jellyfish *still* can't swim!

A HIDING PLACE

A baby kangaroo knows what to do when a dangerous enemy comes near. He dives head first into the pouch on his mother's tummy. He can jump in even if his mother is hopping. Then, safe in the pouch, he turns around and pokes out his head to see where his mom is going. He trusts his mother's protection. She protects him, and herself, with her strong hind legs. She can use them to kick an enemy and to get away quickly. The baby kangaroo knows his mother's pouch is the safest place to be.

Very few parents have pouches. God gives parents to animals and people to help protect them, but God Himself is a person's best protector. In the Bible, King David calls God his "hiding place." Even though King David faced many problems and fought many battles, he knew God was with him, no matter what. He trusted God's protection.

If you are afraid of something—maybe you fear the dark, or you're nervous about a new situation, or there's a bully in your class—ask God to be your hiding place and your protector. God doesn't have a pouch for you to hide in, but He's always glad when you dive into prayer and ask for His help. He promises always to be there for you. And no thing or person is as strong as God.

Rescue me from my enemies, O Lord, for I hide myself in you.
– PSALMS 143:9

WHEN YOU PRAY

Thank God for loving you and always being with you as your Helper, Protector and Friend. Ask Him to help you remember to pray to Him when you are afraid.

REMEMBER

When you are afraid,
You can ask God in prayer
To help and protect you,
'Cause God's always there.

SEAWEED GIFT

Do you like getting presents? Birthday gifts, Christmas presents or special surprises are always fun to receive. But what if someone brought you a piece of seaweed or a bottle cap as a gift? If you were a flightless cormorant, a big bird who can't fly, you would like it. The flightless cormorant lives in a seaweed nest on the rocky shores of the Galapagos Islands in the Pacific Ocean. When the male walks back to the nest after diving in the sea for food, he brings the female a piece of seaweed, a bottle cap or strand of rope he's found to add to the nest. She likes that. Lots of creatures—even spiders—give gifts to each other, but they're not the kind of gifts we humans would like.

God knows just what sorts of gifts we humans like and need. And the Bible calls God the Giver of every good and perfect gift. God gives you your unique personality, your smile, your talents, your family, your friends. Creation—the whole world—is a gift from God for us to use, care for and enjoy. God's most important gift to us is Jesus, His Son. God wants us to accept His gift by asking Jesus into our heart—to forgive us and lead us and be our Friend. Jesus is a gift that lasts forever!

Thanks be to God for His indescribable gift!"
– 2 CORINTHIANS 9:15

WHEN YOU PRAY

Thank God for all
He has given you—
especially Jesus.

REMEMBER

If you got seaweed,
You might make a fuss,
But God gives a Gift that's perfect for us.
That Gift is Jesus,
Who died in our place offering forgiveness
To our human race.

A GULPING HELLO

Ducks spend much of their time in the water, swimming and diving to get fish to eat. Perhaps sometimes they get thirsty. But most of the time, the reason a duck takes a drink is to greet another duck. When one duck swims or waddles up to another, the welcoming duck takes a swallow of water to say hello and give a sign of peace.

Like animals, people have their own methods of greeting. We smile, shake hands and speak to each other. Maybe we hug or kiss. Being friendly, kind and welcoming is important. Jesus taught us to be kind to everyone. He visited and healed people that others ignored or left out. Poor, sick, disabled and unfortunate people were very important to Jesus. He loved them. In fact Jesus said, "I tell you the truth, whatever you did for one of the least of these brothers of mine, you did for me."(Matthew 25:40)

Do you have someone in your school, neighborhood or church who needs welcoming? Has a new kid joined your class, or does someone have a difference that makes her feel left out? What can you do to make that person feel welcome? Can you draw her a picture? Invite him over? Sit by her? By giving these signs of peace, you are showing Jesus' love for others, and Jesus likes that.

For this very reason, make every effort to add to your faith goodness…
and brotherly kindness… – 2 PETER 1: 5, 7

WHEN YOU PRAY	REMEMBER
Ask God to help you show brotherly kindness to people (and animals).	Although you don't have Webbed feet or a bill, Your welcome's important And part of God's will.

ON THE MARCH

Army ants march along together in search of food. We often think of ants as annoying insects that spoil our picnics, but in South America, army ants are welcome in homes. As the ants march in, people move out of their houses. The ants eat up any insects and pests in the house, and then they march out again. When they're gone, the people move back in.

Sometimes in their travels army ants come to a body of water they must cross. A group of the ants lock their legs together to make a bridge for the other ants to crawl across. By helping each other and marching together, army ants survive.

Have you ever held hands with someone to cross a busy street? Have you held hands in a circle to pray? Maybe you've joined hands with someone who pulled you along on roller skates or ice skates. When we join together with the right people, we are safer and stronger, and we have more fun.

That's why having a church is important. In church, we not only worship God together, but we also help, support and enjoy each other. We can reach out together to serve others. The church makes up the army of God.

You can make your church stronger by praying for your minister or saving some of your allowance for the offering plate. You can make a bridge to your church by inviting friends who don't have a church to be a part of your church family. Anytime you help others, you are a helpful part of God's army.

Two are better than one... – ECCLESIASTES 4:9

WHEN YOU PRAY

Ask God to help you to join with others to do helpful things and make up a strong army for Him.

REMEMBER

Army ants work together,
And that makes them strong.
The church is God's army.
Let's all get along!

PLAYING DEAD?

A 'possum plays dead when she is threatened. She rolls over on her side with her mouth open and her eyes looking lifeless. That's how she "plays possum" to make her attacker lose interest. Then once the attacker leaves, the 'possum scurries away.

When Jesus died on the cross, his Roman enemies wanted to be sure He wasn't just pretending to be dead. So, they stuck a sword in His side to be sure. Jesus was dead. But then Jesus did the biggest miracle ever. He surprised everyone by rising from His grave three days later. His resurrection proved that He was God, just as He said. That miracle made all of His sad, doubting disciples very happy!

After He rose, Jesus walked around on earth and showed Himself not just to His eleven disciples, but also to hundreds of other people. He talked with friends and cooked a meal on the beach for His disciples. He wasn't a ghost. People could touch Him, yet He could walk through walls and appear and disappear. For forty days, He showed that He was miraculously alive again. His followers couldn't wait to tell everyone far and wide Jesus' good news. Then, as His disciples watched, Jesus rose on a cloud into heaven to be with God. He promised He'd prepare a place there for each of us!

When Jesus rose early on the first day of the week, He appeared first to Mary Magdalene....Afterward Jesus appeared in a different form to two of them while they were walking in the country. Later Jesus appeared to the eleven as they were eating...
— MARK 16:9-14

WHEN YOU PRAY	REMEMBER
Thank God that Jesus made a way for you to live with God forever in heaven.	A 'possum knows how to play Dead as a trick To make all her enemies leave. But Jesus really died on His enemy's cross, Then rose, so that all would believe.

BIG EARS

The fennec, the world's smallest fox, lives in the hot, dry deserts of Africa and Arabia. She's the smallest of all the foxes in size, but she has the biggest ears. Her ears help her to hear, but they come in handy for another reason, too. They help keep her cool. God specially designed the fennec's ears to give off heat, and that keeps the Fennec from getting too uncomfortable in a hot climate.

We see large ears on people, too. But whatever size human ears come in, they aren't used for staying cool. They're for hearing. Deaf people, who cannot hear, can listen by using their eyes as if they were ears. They watch people's lips or hand motions to see what they are saying. That way they can listen and understand what's going on. When Jesus lived on earth, He healed deaf people He met, because He wanted them to be able to listen to Him as He told them important truths about God.

Many things Jesus said are written in the Bible. He told people He was God's Son, and He was the Way to God and to life in heaven. Some people listened and believed. Some people, however, would not believe what Jesus said.

Jesus called those people "deaf," because even though they had ears that worked, they would not listen to His truth. Today, just as in that day, Jesus wants us to hear His truth and believe in Him.

If anyone has ears to hear, let him hear.
– MARK 4:23

WHEN YOU PRAY

Ask God to give you ears
that hear His truth.

REMEMBER

Whatever the size or the shape
Of your ears,
You can be one of the people who hears.
Listen to Jesus' words of God's love.
He and His words lead to heaven above.

WALKING STICK

Have you ever seen a walking stick? This little insect looks just like a twig! If you look closely, you'll see it has six legs, two eyes and two antennae, and it may have two wings as well. It can be brown, gray, green or tan, depending on the bush or tree it lives in and eats. God designed the walking stick to mimic the plant it lives on. It so closely matches its surroundings that, even when it is walking, it looks like a small branch blowing in the wind. That's good protection. By mimicking the plant, the walking stick is hidden from creatures that would eat it.

If you find one of these little insects, put it on your finger. It won't bite. It's fun to see how its tiny claws help it hang onto you, even when you turn it upside down.

God created His people to mimic in a special way, very different from what the walking stick does. We are to mimic God, doing things the way Jesus would. Instead of helping us blend in or hide, mimicking God's way makes us stick out in the world. Then others know that we belong to Him.

When you tell the truth or take up for someone who is being bullied, you are mimicking Jesus. And Jesus promises His way is right and best. He says that if we ask, He will help us to walk His way, even if others think we are walking upside down!

This is what the Lord says: …Ask where the good way is, and walk in it.
– JEREMIAH 6:16

WHEN YOU PRAY

Ask God to show you ways you can honor Him and stick up or stick out for Him.

REMEMBER

God made some insects to do a cool trick:
To hide in disguise like a thin walking stick.
But God tells His people: "Don't hide!
You stand out."
Walk in God's ways even when
Others doubt.

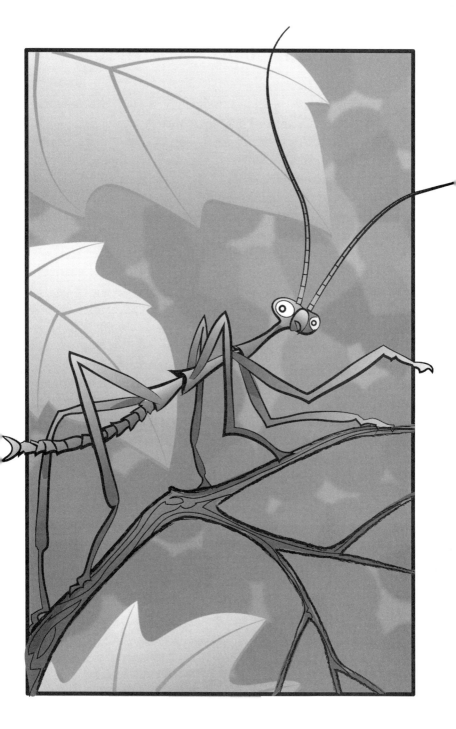

ARMS, LEGS AND TAILS

*F*urry squirrels use their long, bushy tails for many things. When they scamper up trees or play chase with each other, you might see their tails up, or down or twitching. A tree squirrel uses his tail for balance when walking on a high wire or jumping from limb to limb. A ground squirrel uses his for signaling another squirrel. In cold areas, a squirrel will wrap his tail around his body to keep warm. In the desert, a squirrel uses his for a sunshade. In fact, the word squirrel means *shadow tail*.

God creates animals with useful parts to their bodies, and each part—like the squirrel's tail—does something different. All the parts of a human body are useful, too. Our hands do one thing; our feet do another. Our eyes, ears, nose and mouth have different jobs, but they're all parts of the same body.

The Bible says people who believe in Jesus are "the body of Christ." It means we are to work together with our different strengths to help each other. Maybe you're an "arm" who helps someone work, or an "ear" who listens well. Maybe you're a "heart" who loves others and enjoys making them feel good about themselves.

Think about your body and its parts. What part of the body of Christ do you think you are? Ask your parents what they think, too. Then use your gifts and your life for God.

God has arranged the parts in the body, every one of them, just as He wanted them to be...there are many parts ...Now you are the body of Christ, and each one of you is a part of it." – 1 CORINTHIANS 12:18, 27

WHEN YOU PRAY

Ask God to show you how to use your gifts so that you can do your part for the body of Christ.

REMEMBER

Whatever you look like,
You're someone God chose.
You serve as His body, and only He knows
The best way to use you.
So give Him control, and trust that He'll help you
Succeed in your role.

RUNNING CUCKOO

Have you ever seen the "Road Runner" cartoons? Unlike the cartoon character, roadrunners are real birds that can run up to 25 mph. They are members of the cuckoo family. The roadrunner got his name in the old days from his habit of running on the road alongside a horse drawn wagon. The roadrunner liked to eat insects that flew up when the horses' hooves thudded by. Today, roadrunners still run on the road, but they must dart in front of faster moving vehicles. Then they rush to safety in the grass.

Even though a roadrunner can fly, he likes it best to be on the ground. In fact, one of his nicknames is "ground cuckoo."

Like the roadrunner, people like speed, too. We have fast cars, fast food, fast computers and a fast life. Sometimes our rushed life may even make us feel a little cuckoo! Although it's hard to be still and quiet in our hurried world, the Bible tells us God wants us to take time out to be still and talk with Him.

You can choose any time for your quiet time—maybe you pray just after you crawl into bed at night. Perhaps you are even reading this book in bed right now. Maybe just before you get up in the morning, you can take a minute to tell God you love Him and ask Him to guide you though your day. Whenever you choose to be still and focus on God, you are honoring Him.

Be still and know that I am God."
– PSALM 46:10

WHEN YOU PRAY

Ask God to help you set aside time to be still and know He is God.

REMEMBER

Although it may seem life's road is a race,
The Lord wants us each to
Slow down our pace
And focus on Him, His love and His grace.

LIVING NIGHT LIGHTS

*H*ave you ever gone outside on a summer night and seen lightning bugs—fireflies—flickering in the darkness? A firefly blinks its light in its abdomen to attract a mate. The blink is made when special chemicals in the bug's body mix together. The female firefly answers the male's blink with her own blink until they find each other. They can locate each other because each light stands out in the darkness.

Sometimes, certain types of fireflies get together with others in groups, so they can all flash their lights at the same time. Putting their little lights together, they can be seen a long way off.

Jesus is called a Light in the Bible. Long before it happened, when God's prophets told people that Jesus would come, they described Him as a Light in the darkness. And when Jesus came, He lit the way to God by showing people God's power and love and by saving us from our sins.

Because light attracts attention, God tells us to be lights, too. He wants us to attract others to Him. But God didn't create us with stomachs that light up. Instead, He made us able to do good deeds, love others and tell them about Jesus. That's the way we stand out in the world. And when we get together with other Christians, we can make an even bigger difference. We can shine brightly for God!

Let your light so shine before men that they may see your good deeds and praise your Father in heaven.
– MATTHEW 5:20

WHEN YOU PRAY	REMEMBER
Ask God to help you light the way for others to find Him.	Your love is a light that can Shine really bright. It's yours to show others All day and at night.

PELICAN POUCH

A pelican is a large odd-looking bird with webbed feet and a long beak. She has a pouch under her bill where she stores fish, her main food. Some pelicans swim along scooping up fish with their beaks and storing them in the pouch. Some fly through the air and dive straight down to the water, snatching a fish that way. The pouch stretches as it fills, and the pelican can keep lots of fish in there. So when she's hungry, there's plenty to eat!

Human beings can store things, too, in something much better than a pelican pouch. In our brain, we can store all the information we want to—our brain never gets full. Do you know your phone number and address? Do you remember facts you learned from books or things your parents told you? Once you learn something, your brain keeps that information forever, so that you can use it when you need it.

When we fill our mind with God's word by reading the Bible and learning verses from it, we are storing up the most important thing—God's truth. God's word is "food" for our soul. The Bible's truths do more than tell us how to act. Its verses also comfort us when we feel sad, alone or angry. People in the Bible had all the same feelings you have. That's why you can always find something written in the Bible that can be helpful to you. Why don't you store up a verse today?

For the word of the Lord is right and true…
– PSALM 33:4

WHEN YOU PRAY

Ask God to help you learn a verse from the Bible today. (Perhaps you'll want to start by learning the one on this page!)

REMEMBER

If you were a pelican, you would store fish.
You'd have a big pouch and eat
when you wish.
But, God made your storehouse
the brain which will hold
the treat of God's truth.
And it never grows old.

PHONY FRILLS

A frilled lizard, who lives in deserts and the dry grasslands of Australia, has a trick that protects him. When an enemy comes near, he takes the skin on his neck, called his frills, and spreads it wide, pretending to be much bigger and fiercer than he is. Looking big, he scares his enemies away. Then, the frilled lizard shrinks back down to his real size.

Sometimes people try to look big and important in front of other people. They want everyone to think they are powerful. Sometimes people do that by bragging, or by saying unkind things to make someone else feel small. Or they act pushy or bossy. These are the way they puff themselves up. But those are phony frills.

Jesus tells us that showing off doesn't make us important. When Jesus' disciples argued among themselves about which of them was to be greatest (Luke 2:24), Jesus told them that in order to be great, they must be like servants. Another time, they asked Jesus, "Who is the greatest in the kingdom of heaven?" Jesus brought a little child out of the crowd. He told them they must become like little children. "Whoever humbles himself like this child is the greatest in the kingdom of heaven (Matthew 18:4)," Jesus said.

Humbling yourself means making someone else feel important. If you're humble, you'll be friendly, even to unpopular people. You won't brag—except maybe a little to your parents—when you do something outstanding. You'll thank God for your successes, since He gave you your talents. When we make ourselves small, Jesus makes us great.

Whoever humbles himself like this child is the greatest in the kingdom of heaven. — MATTHEW 18:4

WHEN YOU PRAY	REMEMBER
Ask God to help you make someone else feel important today.	Jesus, the Master, the greatest of all, Says we are the biggest when We become small.

SOGGY FEATHERS

*T*he sand grouse is a bird who carries water to his chicks in an unusual way. The male has fluffy breast feathers, so he uses them like a sponge to soak up water. He wades into a pool, lets the feathers take up the water, and then flies back to the nest. The chicks suck the water from his soggy feathers. A sand grouse might fly more than 60 miles a day just to find water to take back to the nest.

Animals and people must have water to live. We get thirsty without it. Even Jesus got thirsty. But Jesus knows that people thirst in another way besides just feeling dry in their throat and mouth. They thirst in their spirit for God's love, peace, hope and forgiveness. Jesus came so that people would never thirst this way again. He wanted people to soak up God's love through Him. He called Himself "living water."

When people take Him inside themselves by accepting Him as their Savior, then His love, forgiveness, hope and strength bubble up inside them. Jesus' "water" is even better than a rushing spring, because He never runs dry!

You can carry a cool drink to someone you know who seems hot and thirsty—your postman or a parent who is working hard outside. But the best water to carry is Jesus' "living water," which you share when you tell someone about Him.

Whoever drinks the water I give him will never thirst.
– JOHN 4:10, 14

WHEN YOU PRAY	REMEMBER
Think of someone you know who doesn't know Jesus. Ask God to help you carry Jesus' love to that person.	A sand grouse might slurp from his Father's wet chest, But we'd rather drink from a cup. When spirits are thirsty, Christ's water is best. And He wants to fill us all up!

THE BEST PRIZE TO PACK

*P*ack rats who live in the deserts of the Southwest think that a prickly cactus clump is a comfortable spot to live. They build their grass-lined nests there, because no enemies want to come in. But a prickly pear pack rat must be careful where she puts her feet when she's scurrying in and out of her home.

A pack rat darts in and out, because she is curious. She is always on the look-out for something bright and interesting. When she finds a shiny nail, a bright stone or some other small object, she will scamper home with it or hide it. She packs in all the shiny things she can find—that's how she got her name. Sometimes, carrying a prize home, a pack rat will find something even better. She will drop the first item and take home the new one instead.

People can be like pack rats. We like pretty things. Sometimes people gather treasures until their houses are full. But Jesus warns us not to put too much of our time and money into earthly things, because those don't last. He says if we love and serve God and help others, then we will get treasure in heaven that lasts forever. It's worth dropping earthly things to pick up the best kind of treasure—God's kind.

Do not store up for yourselves treasures on earth, where moth and rust destroy and where thieves break in and steal. But store up for yourselves treasures in heaven…
— MATTHEW:6:19-20

WHEN YOU PRAY

Thank God for the earthly treasures He has given you. Ask Him to show you how you can share with people in need, so that you can use your treasures to serve Him.

REMEMBER

The Bible says not to store Treasures on earth. It's treasure in heaven that Offers true worth.

FROG IN YOUR THROAT?

*F*rogs come in a variety of colors and sizes. The Goliath frog of Africa is nearly a foot long, and the smallest frog grows to only half an inch. But one of the things frogs have in common is that almost all males have a voice. They mainly use it to call to females during the mating season.

To call, the frog forces air from his lungs across his vocal cords, which vibrate and give off a sound. Some frogs also have a big vocal sac in their throat. It swells up to a great size and helps the frog call more loudly. Perhaps you've heard the strange croaks and sounds frogs make.

What other sounds do you hear when you go outside? Almost all creatures talk to each other in some way. Birds twitter, dogs bark, cattle bellow, lambs bleat. Roosters crow, crickets chirp, cats meow. Sometimes it can get very noisy.

God gave most people the ability to make sounds, too. He made each person's voice different. You have a voiceprint (sort of like a fingerprint) that is all yours. No one else has a print exactly like it. Can you sing? Some people have beautiful singing voices, and some can't carry a tune. But even if we can only "make a joyful noise unto the Lord," God wants us to use what He's given us to praise Him and share His Word from the Bible. How can you use your voice for Him today?

They raise their voices, they shout for joy;...they acclaim the Lord's majesty.
— ISAIAH 24:14

WHEN YOU PRAY	REMEMBER
Tell God how much you love Him or sing a song to Him.	Your voice is much better Than that of a frog Or a cow, a rooster, a cat or a dog. So use it for God and sing Out His praise Tell of His goodness and Wonderful ways.

A FLIP OF THE TONGUE

A chameleon is a short, flat lizard who can do some amazing things. He can change colors quickly from green, yellow or white to brown or black. He can become spotted or blotched. His eyes stick out, and each eye can move without the other; so the chameleon can look forward and backward at the same time. Instead of clinging with sharp claws like most other lizards, a chameleon's feet grasp like hands. He also has a grasping tail.

Most chameleons live in trees and have a long, sticky tongue to capture a tasty bug for dinner. The tongue may be as long as the chameleon's entire body. The chameleon has good aim, and his tongue shoots out so quickly that the human eye can hardly see it. The chameleon himself moves slowly, so it's a good thing he has a quick tongue.

No matter how many other amazing things the chameleon can do, it's very important that he be able to control his tongue, since that's how he eats. The Bible says controlling the tongue is important for people, too. But not for catching bugs! The Bible means we should watch what we say. Our words can be used for good or for bad. God wants us to use them for good. You can do that by encouraging a friend, telling that person what you like about him. You can use your tongue for saying thank you. If you've said the wrong words and hurt someone's feelings, you can make it better by saying, "I'm sorry."

Self-control means controlling the tongue! A quick retort can ruin everything.
— PROVERBS 13:3 THE LIVING BIBLE

WHEN YOU PRAY

Ask God to help you control your tongue and make your words helpful and kind.

REMEMBER

Chameleon's quick tongue is
To help him catch prey,
But your tongue makes words,
So watch what you say!

TRAVELING ARMOR

A turtle can live almost anywhere that isn't cold all year—in deserts or rivers, grasslands or the sea. Turtles are reptiles, and they are the only creatures of their kind with a shell. The turtle's shell is like a suit of armor, protecting her from enemies. Most turtles can pull their head, legs and tail safely into their shell, closing their shell tightly behind them. A turtle doesn't have to move fast to run away, because she escapes by hiding in her shell.

Some turtles, known as softshell turtles, can't withdraw into their shell. But they are fast. Unlike their slow brothers and sisters, the smooth softshell turtle of North America can outrun a man on level ground. They have to be fast, because their soft shell won't protect them from enemies. Only hard armor allows a turtle to stand her ground.

People don't carry armor on their backs, but the Bible tells of an invisible armor for God's people that we carry in our spirit. It is the armor of God. It doesn't cover our body; it covers our spirit—our heart and mind—to keep out evil. If someone stabs at you with unkind words, you can protect your heart by putting on this special armor—the knowledge of God's truth that says you are special, and He loves you.

When we read and believe the Bible, when we trust Jesus and when we pray for God's help and peace, we are putting on our invisible armor. And we can put it on anytime we need it, to stand our ground for Jesus! In Ephesians 6:14-17 you can read a wonderful description of the armor of God.

Therefore put on the full armor of God, so that when the day of evil comes, you may be able to stand your ground..." — EPHESIANS 6:13.

WHEN YOU PRAY

Thank God for His protection and ask Him to help you put on His armor every day.

REMEMBER

A turtle can use the hard shell on her back,
To serve as her armor—
A kind that we lack.
But you, as God's child,
Have His armor—the best!
Invisible safety that beats all the rest!

THE PUZZLING PLATYPUS

What shy animal has a bill like a duck, a furry covering like a mole, flat webbed feet with claws and a beaver-like tail? The answer is… platypus (which means "flat foot"), a strange-looking animal found only in Australia. The platypus not only has parts that look like they came from different kinds of animals, but she also behaves like different creatures. She hatches from an egg, like a reptile or bird; but she is furry and drinks her mother's milk, like a mammal. She's a mammal, by the way. A platypus spends lots of time under water hunting for food, but she lives in a burrow under the ground. The platypus doesn't mind being unusual. She makes use of all the things God equipped her with to survive in an ever-changing world.

Sometimes we wonder why God made animals the way He did. And sometimes we wonder why He made us a certain way. Perhaps we feel too big or too small, or we wish we had a different nose or eyes or skin color. Maybe we don't feel like we fit in with everyone else. Whatever you look like, God custom designed you. He made you uniquely you for a purpose, which He will help you discover if you ask Him.

The Bible explains that God knows exactly how many hairs you have on your head (Luke 12:7), and He knows to the very day how long your life will be (Psalms 139:13-16). He knows what He will do through you to make this world a better place. You are very special to God, and He loves you exactly as you are!

I praise you because I am fearfully and wonderfully made.

— PSALM 139:14

WHEN YOU PRAY

Thank God for how He made you. Ask Him to show you how to use your life to praise and serve Him.

REMEMBER

Some creatures look strange,
But there isn't a doubt
That God has good reasons we've
Not figured out.
Though people can't know God's
Mysterious ways,
We each should still give Him our
Thanks and our praise.

UPSIDE DOWN, SWIMMIN' AROUND

*I*n fresh water in tropical Africa, you might see an Upside Down Catfish. He swims right side up, then upside down, and then he flips again—over and over.

Perhaps you like to hang upside down on a jungle gym. Maybe you've been upside down on a roller coaster. It's fun for a while, but then it becomes uncomfortable, and you want to be right side up again. Maybe that's what the Upside Down Catfish thinks, too.

Sometimes our feelings seem upside down, and it doesn't feel good. Even though we may be right side up on the outside, when bad things happen, it seems like everything is turned over the wrong way. If parents divorce, or friends are mean to us, or someone we love dies, we don't believe our lives can ever be right side up again.

In the Bible, many people cried out to God when things got bad, scary or sad. God always helped them, even though sometimes they had to wait for God's timing for things to change. While He was on earth, Jesus reached out to everyone who called to Him. He will help you, too, if you ask Him. He can give you strength and peace and hope. He can send a friend to help you through hard times. If you are having any kind of trouble, turn to God. He knows just how to turn your life right side up again at just the right time.

He heals the brokenhearted and binds up their wounds.

— PSALM 147:3

WHEN YOU PRAY

Thank God for the good
things in your life and
ask Him to help you
through the bad times.

REMEMBER

Both catfish and people can turn upside down.
So how can we make a smile from a frown?
By turning things over to God when we pray,
We'll find He sends comfort and
Help for each day.

HUNTING BY EAR

Did you know a tiger hunts by using his ears? A tiger has a weak sense of smell and sight. If something is sitting still, he can't tell if it's an animal or a bush. He listens carefully for the sound of movement, and then he uses his speed and strength to chase after whatever moved.

The tiger doesn't worry about what he can't do. He just does what he can. We can learn something from the tiger. Sometimes we spend too much time fretting about things we can't do well. We get frustrated if we're not good in a sport or can't make as good a grade in school as another person. Sometimes we get discouraged, comparing ourselves to someone else.

However, no matter how strong or smart another person seems, every person has some kind of weakness. The only perfect person who has ever lived was Jesus. Each person has some kind of strength or gift, too. Hard work and practice help you develop that gift, and God helps, too. The Bible says, "Whatever your hand finds to do, do it with all your might, as unto God (Colossians 3:23)." Instead of worrying about what you can't do, work with all your might on what you can do. Then do it for others and for God.

If you can't find your strength inside yourself, ask God to show it to you or fill you with His strength.

…I showed you that by this kind of hard work we must help the weak, remembering the words the Lord Jesus Himself said: "It is more blessed to give than to receive." — ACTS 20:35

WHEN YOU PRAY

Ask God to help you with things you feel weak in. Ask Him to show you what you do best, and then do it for Him.

REMEMBER

You may be weak, but with God you are strong! Do what you can and help others along.

GAGGLE AND COO

Many creatures stick together in groups to help each other, protect each other or keep each other company. Each different collection of animals has a name. You may have heard some of them: a *school* of fish, a *herd* of cattle, a *gaggle* of geese or a *swarm* of bees. However, did you know about a *crusher* of rhinoceros, a *pride* of lions, a *stripe* of zebras, a *coo* of pigeons or a *charm* of hummingbirds? Those are funny group names, aren't they?

Whatever their group is called, animals like to be together with their kind. People like to be together, too. God gave us each other, because He said, "It is not good for man to be alone." The first people, Adam and Eve, created the first group of people—a family.

Who is in your family? Whether you have a family of your own, or you have someone who takes care of you that you are not related to, you are also part of a larger family—God's family. God is your Father who loves you. Jesus calls Himself your Brother. Those who love Jesus are brothers and sisters in Christ. In a group of Jesus-followers, we all have the same name: we're a church of Christians!

Jesus said, "Whoever does the will of my Father in heaven is my brother and sister and mother."
— MATTHEW 12: 50

WHEN YOU PRAY

Thank God for your family
and for being your loving
Heavenly Father.

REMEMBER

You're not in a charm,
Or a gaggle or coo.
No, you're in a family,
God's family, too.

HIPPETY WALK?

The green tree frog of the Southern United States is less than two inches long. He has a bold stripe that runs along his side. His pretty green color blends in with leaves. Like most frogs, tree frogs jump using their long, strong back legs. The green tree frog has strong back legs and could leap eight to ten feet if he chose. However, unlike other frogs, he prefers to walk or climb instead of hop. He looks like other frogs, but he has his own way of doing things.

People have their own ways of doing things, too. Do you know someone who acts or talks differently from you? When someone has unusual habits, he often faces teasing or unkind words from others. Jesus faced that. Because He was God's Son, Jesus was unlike anyone else who ever walked the earth. Jesus taught people to forgive others instead of getting even. He showed people how to stop trying to be first and how to be a servant instead. He befriended people that no one else would befriend. He wasn't afraid to do things differently, because He was doing things God's way.

It takes courage to follow Jesus, because people may tease us and make us feel as odd as a green tree frog. But that's O.K. God says when we do things His way, even though it is different from the way of the world, He will reward us.

I have no greater joy than to hear that my children are walking in the truth.
— JOHN 1:4

WHEN YOU PRAY

Ask God for the courage to be different.

REMEMBER

The world's full of those who may
Hop the wrong way.
But you can still walk in Christ's
Steps every day—
'Cause that is a difference God says is O.K.!

CLOWNING AROUND

*L*ots of creatures in nature work together for protection and food. In the sea, the clownfish likes to live with the sea anemone. The clownfish feeds and hides in the long finger-like tentacles of the anemone. The anemone doesn't mind, because the clownfish acts as a lure to other fish. When a hungry fish comes to eat the clownfish, the hungry fish becomes the sea anemone's meal instead!

The fish called the Pacific cleaner wrasse is another example of fishy cooperation. He eats harmful parasites off of larger fish. Normally, the larger fish would eat the wrasse. But because the wrasse is getting rid of the bloodsuckers that bother the big fish, she leaves the wrasse alone.

People also work best when we cooperate. Do you ever help your parents around the house? The more helpers there are, the less work each person has to do. At church, do you put some of your money in the offering plate? Even small amounts grow as others add to it, and that money can be used to feed the hungry or help the sick. Even though you are not an anemone, you can help protect someone like your little brother or sister. You can team up with others for all kinds of things.

Two are better than one, because they have a good return for their work.
— ECCLESIATES 1:9

WHEN YOU PRAY

Thank God that He is always your teammate, even if no one else is around.

REMEMBER

Two are more fun for
Clowning around,
Or sharing God's work
Wherever it's found.

WHO STAYS THE SAME?

Change is all around us. Caterpillars turn into butterflies; snakes shed their skins. Deer grow horns and lose them again. Baby animals leave their mothers and learn to hunt for their own food. Plants grow and develop, and so do you. Even the earth itself changes— mountains push up or get worn down, rivers dig deeper channels or dry up. Crashing waves eat away at cliffs along the sea. Stars burn out. Yet, no matter what else changes, God does not.

Only God and His truth are the same yesterday, today, tomorrow and forever. In the Bible God describes Himself in many ways: He's the Creator of everything. He speaks to the sea and controls it. He tells the morning when to dawn. He is powerful and knows all things. Nothing in heaven or on earth would work without Him. God is perfect, and He hates sin and wickedness. He loves truth. God tells us many more things about Himself in the Bible, but one of the best things is that He wants to be our Friend. That never changes, either, even when we sometimes disappoint God with how we act.

Jesus makes it possible for each of us to be God's friend, because He took the punishment for every one of our sins. If we believe that He is God's Son who died for us and rose from the dead, and if we ask Him to forgive us our sins, He will come into our heart. And He will never leave. Not ever! Because God says it, we can count on it.

I the Lord do not change.

— MALACHI 2:6

WHEN YOU PRAY

Thank God that because of Jesus' forgiveness, we can be friends with Him forever.

REMEMBER

God is forever. His love Never ends. He never changes. He's made us His friends.

MONKEY SEE, MONKEY DO

Monkeys learn from each other. A whole group may copy some activity they see another monkey doing. A two-year-old Japanese Macaque monkey named Imo discovered that washing her sweet potatoes before eating them took off the gritty dirt. It made them taste better. Soon her whole group began washing their potatoes.

Sometimes, however, monkeys will see another monkey misbehave, and they will act the same way, such as throwing things at others. That's when monkeying around is not a good thing.

Whether you know it or not, your friends and playmates are watching you. They see what you do, and sometimes they'll copy it. That's why your example is important. Forgiving others, being kind, telling the truth, working hard, going to church—all those actions are good things for others to imitate.

Jesus gave us His example to follow. He was the only perfect leader ever born, because He was God's only Son. Jesus knows we can't be perfect. But He tells us to do our best to copy how He acted, and He will help us become good leaders, too.

I AM THE LORD YOUR GOD … BE HOLY, BECAUSE I AM HOLY.
– LEVITICUS 11:44

WHEN YOU PRAY

Ask God to help you be a good example for others to follow.

REMEMBER

Don't monkey around doing things
That are wrong.
Instead, let your deeds show to
Whom you belong.
When leading for good, doing all
That you should,
You show that with Jesus you're
Loving and strong.

TOUCHY, TOUCHY!

All creatures from small to large have one sense in common—the sense of touch. For spiders, a vibrating web means they've caught something tasty for dinner. Sometimes we call a bug's antennae "feelers," because they're used for feeling. For example, flies and honeybees use their antennae to detect wind speeds. If they feel the wind is too strong, they know to stay put so they won't be blown backwards when they try to fly. An octopus' tentacles are sensitive to touch. Many close-knit groups of animals will cuddle or nuzzle or lick each other clean, because that touch means friendship.

The sense of touch is important to humans, too. Jesus often put His hand on people when He healed them. Jesus made the blind see, the lame walk, the dumb speak. He even touched and cured people that others thought were untouchable—like people called lepers who had a dreadful skin disease.

Jesus was God's Son in human form. Part of the reason He was born on earth was so people could see Him and touch Him and know that God is real and that He loves us. When He returned to heaven, Jesus promised that even though we can't touch or see Him on earth anymore, He is always with us. And He never breaks a promise.

The Word became flesh and took up residence among us, and we have beheld His glory, the glory of the one and only Son of the Father, full of grace and truth.

— JOHN 1:14

WHEN YOU PRAY

Ask God to help you know Him better, so you will understand He is really with you all the time, even though you can't touch Him.

REMEMBER

God is a spirit we can't feel by touch,
But Jesus was God in man's skin.
He walked among us,
And loved us so much,
That He died on the cross for our sin.

BIG NAMES

All animals have a big name that scientists give them. For instance, a bear's scientific name is *Ursidae carnivora*. The name "bear" is just its common name, which is easier to say. A camel is a *Camelus camelidae*. What is your name? Is your name simpler to say than the scientific name for human beings—*Homo sapiens*?

Names can be easy or hard to say. But no matter what your name is, God knows it. It is not common to Him. It is important, because you are.

In the Bible we're told that Jewish parents gave each child a name that had a certain meaning. For instance, Isaac means laughter. Isaac's mother laughed when God told her she would have a baby, because she was very, very old—ninety years old, in fact. God Himself gave some special people their names before they were born, such as John the Baptist and Jesus. And He changed some of His followers' names after they were grown up, to show that He was doing something special in their lives.

God has a name, too. We know it, because His servant Moses asked what His name was. And God answered, "I AM." Jesus also used that name, because He is one with God (John 8:58).

No matter what your name is or what it means, God knows exactly who you are and what you will become. He made you, He loves you and He has a plan for your life.

He calls His own ... by name and leads them out.
— JOHN 10:3

WHEN YOU PRAY

Thank God that He knows your name
and will lead you through life.

REMEMBER

You could be Mary or Kerri
Or Todd,
Whatever your name,
You're important to God.

UNDERGROUND FARMERS

*E*arthworms have an important job, but they work in secret where we can't see them. As they squiggle and dig underground, they turn over the soil. Plants grow better when earthworms are around, because worms put air and nutrients into the soil when they wiggle through it. Sometimes rain washes a worm to the surface, or we dig one up. But usually we don't see the lowly earthworm doing its quiet work and making things grow better.

The Bible tells us when we do good works—like giving to the needy—we should try to do it without being seen by others, too. Have you ever done a hidden, underground job? One way to do that is to be a "secret pal" and leave a little surprise at an elderly shut-in's door. Or, save your allowance and give it to a charity without telling anyone what you gave. God sees everything that we do in secret. Even when we hide away and pray behind closed doors, God sees and hears us. In fact He encourages people to pray in secret (Matthew 6: 5-6). And He promises to reward us in heaven for every good deed we do that no one else sees.

> … give to the poor in secret. Your Father, who sees
> what is done in secret, will reward you.
> — MATTHEW 6:4 COMMON ENGLISH BIBLE

WHEN YOU PRAY

Ask God to show you
someone you can secretly
help or cheer up.

REMEMBER

Under earth's surface,
The lowly earthworms
Help all the plants with their
Wiggles and squirms.
You can help too with a secret good deed.
Reach out today to a friend who's in need!

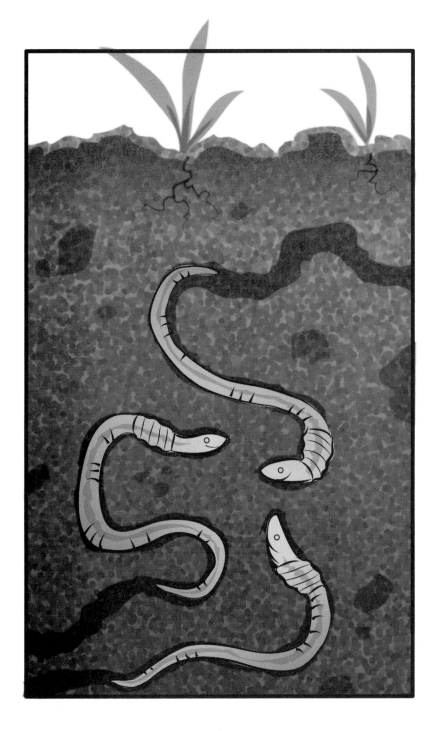

WHAT DID YOU SAY?

Most of God's creatures communicate with each other in some way—whistling, howling, buzzing, squeaking or making other sounds. Scientists study animals to learn more about how they talk to each other without words. And they want to find out how a human might talk with an animal, too. Animal scientists have found that chimpanzees are very smart, but they can't speak in words, because they have different vocal cords than human beings. So, scientists taught chimps how to talk with their hands using sign language. These chimps learned to tell the scientists, "I'm hungry" or "I want to play" and other things. They understood what the scientists signed back to them, too.

God made human beings to communicate with each other and with Him. Mainly we do that with words. God speaks every language. He likes communicating with us. The Bible says that God talked to His servant Moses on a mountain. There He gave Moses the Ten Commandments, laws for His people to follow. God spoke to many characters in the Bible. He also put His words in the mouths of messengers called prophets, who then told God's people what He said.

The Bible is full of God's words that He inspired special people to write for Him. The Bible helps people to know God better. Even though it was written a long time ago, the Bible was written for you. And one of the things God tells you in it is that He likes to hear your words to Him. He wants you to communicate with Him in prayer.

Therefore, let everyone who is godly pray...
— PSALM 32:6

WHEN YOU PRAY

Thank God for His words to you in the Bible, and for prayer.

REMEMBER

God speaks every language
And wants us to pray.
He's never confused by the
Words we may say.

STINGRAYS NEED LOVE, TOO

A stingray is a flat fish with a long, whip-like tail. Most stingrays live in the warm, shallow parts of the ocean or bays on the sandy bottom. Near the middle of the stingray's tail are one or two sharp spines that have barbs on them. If a swimmer disturbs the stingray, he swings up his tail. Poison in the barb makes a painful wound that can be dangerous. You don't want to get near a stingray.

But stingrays who are not threatened, such as those in an open aquarium, can be quite friendly. Some aquariums sell sardines for people to feed their stingrays. There, a stingray will slurp the sardine out of a person's fingers, then flop his flat body up over the side of the aquarium glass to get a nose rub or back rub. People may feel afraid at first, because of the stingray's bad reputation. But once they realize the slick fish is friendly, their fear disappears.

Do you know a kid with a reputation for being mean? Perhaps you know a grumpy grown-up. Our natural reaction is to avoid that person just like a stingray. However, your kindness—like sharing a cookie at the lunch table—can help that person soften up.

Jesus knows it's not easy to act loving toward someone who seems unlovable, so He gives us one way to do it: pretend that person is Him! When we do a nice favor for anyone, Jesus says we're doing that favor for Him.

Whatever you did for one of the least of these brothers of mine, you did for me.
– MATTHEW 25:40

WHEN YOU PRAY	REMEMBER
Ask God for courage to be kind to someone who is not.	When you act with kindness And do the right thing, You help to show others they Don't need to sting.

GREEN BLOOD?

*I*nsects are very different from people. They have blood, but it's not red—it's usually light green, yellow or colorless. They don't have lungs like you do, either. They breathe through tiny holes along their sides. And they don't hear through ears like yours: crickets hear through tiny openings in their front legs, and an ant hears through hairs on its antennae. An insect may have many eyes, but their eyes are always open, because they have no eyelids. Insects buzz, hum or sing in various ways—like flapping their wings fast or rubbing their legs together. But they don't have vocal cords like yours.

And you can't sprout wings like an insect or eat a tree like one. God didn't make you or any human being that way. The Bible says that God designed everything "according to its kind." That means He made each group of creatures in a special way with a certain type of body and a certain way to live. We human beings are our own kind, not related to bugs or monkeys or any other creature. People are God's most special creation, because He made us to be most like Him and to love Him. Our job is the most important one, too—we are to rule over and take care of God's earth and living things.

God created you exactly like you are for a special reason. How can you use the unique gifts He has given you to help take care of His creation and His people?

God made the wild animals according to their kinds, the livestock according to their kinds and all the creatures that move along the ground according to their kinds. Then God said, "Let us make man in our image, in our likeness, and let them rule … over all the earth." – GENESIS 1:24-26

WHEN YOU PRAY

Ask the Lord to show you what He'd like you to do today to help care for an animal, another person or something in nature.

REMEMBER

As God's special person,
You're one of a kind.
Before forming earth, Jesus
Had you in mind.
You're made for a reason
He'll help you to find.

SEA SHELLS

Have you ever gone to the beach and picked up seashells in different shapes and sizes? Every day, billions of empty sea shells wash up on beaches around the world. Each shell once was a protective covering for a mollusk, the soft animal living inside. After a mollusk dies, its shell is left behind to wash up on the sand. Even though many mollusks die every day, there are still billions living in the oceans and bays. You just don't see them in their shell-house under the sea.

Your body is much better than a shell, but it is your covering. It covers the most important part of you, your spirit—the real you—living inside. Bodies grow old, but spirits don't. The Bible tells us that when a person dies, it is only the outer shell, or body, that is left behind. God made each person's spirit to live forever. So, the spirit just leaves its shell behind and moves to a new address—a place we can't see from earth.

For Christians, the people who love Jesus, the Bible says our new address will be in heaven. And there each of us will have a new covering or "body" that won't ever get old or wear out. Jesus Himself is preparing a special place for us there. He promised that. And He's waiting for all His friends to move in one day and celebrate with Him.

In my Father's house are many rooms… I am going there to prepare a place for you … that you also may be where I am.
– JOHN 14:2-3

WHEN YOU PRAY	REMEMBER
Thank God that He gives you life forever through Jesus.	Your looks and your body are Only your shell. The real you's the spirit inside. That part never dies; it will simply Change homes, Forever with God to abide.

WASHED AND DRIED

*D*id you know a jellyfish can't swim? She just floats along in the sea, catching food in the long, threadlike "legs" that trail behind her. (You don't want to bump into or touch a jellyfish, because she stings with those "legs" or tentacles!) Since she can only float, the jellyfish has to go wherever the current takes her. And sometimes the current takes her where she doesn't want to go.

When a jellyfish gets washed up on the sand, she becomes totally helpless. Since she can't move to get back into the water, the jellyfish just dries up and dies there on the beach.

We can learn a lesson from the wishy-washy jellyfish. Sometimes Christians float along with the crowd and do what others are doing, just because that's the easy thing to do. The Bible tells us not to go along with others just because "everybody's doing it." We need to do what the Bible says is right, even if it means swimming against a tide of people going the other way.

If you go God's way, you won't end up washed up, dried up and out of luck. God's way is best, even if you have to go it alone.

Don't copy the behavior and customs of this world, but be a new and different person with a fresh newness in all you do and think. Then you will learn from your own experience how His ways will really satisfy you.
– ROMANS 12:2 THE LIVING BIBLE

WHEN YOU PRAY	REMEMBER
Ask God to help you go His way, even when others don't.	A jellyfish just floats along 'Til she's washed up on the sand. If you will "swim" and go God's way, You'll like the place you land!

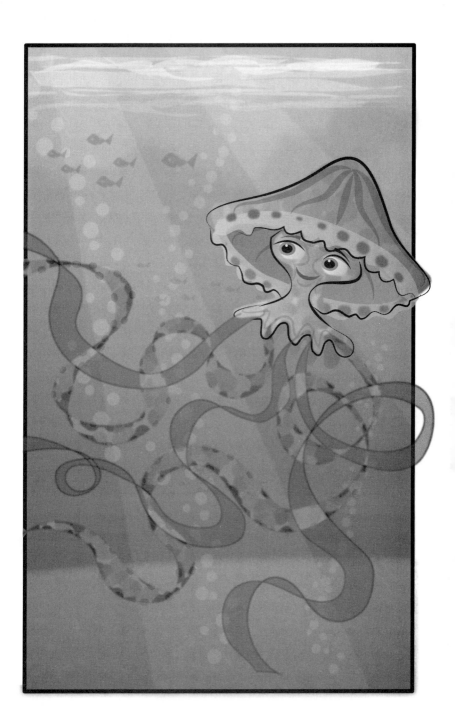

Bible Verse
Index

Acts 20:35 (p. 46) – "In everything I did, I showed you that by this kind of hard work we must help the weak, remembering the words the Lord Jesus himself said: 'It is more blessed to give than to receive.'"

Colossians 3:23 (p. 46) – "Whatever you do, work at it with all your heart, as working for the Lord..."

1 Corinthians 12:18, 27 (p. 22) – "But in fact God has placed the parts in the body, every one of them, just as he wanted them to be."

2 Corinthians 9:15 (p. 10) – "Thanks be to God for his indescribable gift!"

Ecclesiastes 1:9 (p. 52) – "What has been will be again, what has been done will be done again; there is nothing new under the sun."

Ecclesiastes 4:9 (p. 14) – "Two are better than one because they have a good return for their labor..."

Ephesians 6:14-17 (p. 40, p. 41) – "Stand firm then, with the belt of truth buckled around your waist, with the breastplate of righteousness in place, and with your feet fitted with the readiness that comes from the gospel of peace. In addition to all this, take up the shield of faith, with which you can extinguish all the flaming arrows of the evil one. Take the helmet of salvation and the sword of the Spirit, which is the word of God."

Genesis 1:24-26 (p. 68) – "And God said, 'Let the land produce living creatures according to their kinds: the livestock, the creatures that move along the ground, and the wild animals, each according to its kind.' And so it was. God made the wild animals according to their kinds, the livestock according to their kinds, and all the creatures that move along the ground according to their kinds. And God saw that it was good. Then God said, 'Let us make mankind in our image, in our likeness, so that they may rule over the fish in the sea and the birds in the sky, over the livestock and all the wild animals, and over all the creatures that move along the ground.'"

Isaiah 24:14 (p. 36) – "They raise their voices, they shout for joy; from the west they acclaim the Lord's majesty."

Jeremiah 6:16 (p. 20) – "This is what the Lord says: 'Stand at the crossroads and look; ask for the ancient paths, ask where the good way is and walk in it, and you will find rest for your souls.'"

John 1:4 (p. 50) – "In him was life, and that life was the light of all mankind."

John 1:14 (p. 58) – "The Word became flesh and made his dwelling among us. We have seen his glory, the glory of the one and only Son, who came from the Father, full of grace and truth."

John 4:10, 14 (p. 32) – "Jesus answered her, 'If you knew the gift of God and who it is that asks you for a drink, you would have asked him and he would have given you living water... but whoever drinks the water I give them will never thirst. Indeed, the water I give them will become in them a spring of water welling up to eternal life.'"

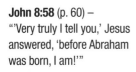

John 8:58 (p. 60) – "'Very truly I tell you,' Jesus answered, 'before Abraham was born, I am!'"

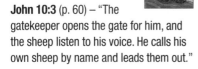

John 10:3 (p. 60) – "The gatekeeper opens the gate for him, and the sheep listen to his voice. He calls his own sheep by name and leads them out."

John 14:2-3 (p. 70) – "My Father's house has many rooms; if that were not so, would I have told you that I am going there to prepare a place for you? And if I go and prepare a place for you, I will come back and

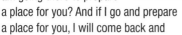

take you to be with me that you also may be where I am."

Leviticus 11:44 (p. 56) – "I am the Lord your God; consecrate yourselves and be holy, because I am holy. Do not make yourselves unclean by any creature that moves along the ground."

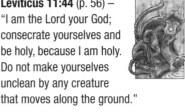

Luke 9:46 (p. 30) – "An argument started among the disciples..."

Luke 12: 7 (p. 42) – "Indeed, the very hairs of your head are all numbered. Don't be afraid; you are worth more than many sparrows."

Malachi 2:6 (p. 54) – "True instruction was in his mouth and nothing false was found on his lips. He walked with me in peace and uprightness, and turned many from sin."

Mark 4:23 (p. 18) – "'If anyone has ears to hear, let them hear.'"

Mark 16:9-14 (p. 16) – "When Jesus rose early on the first day of the week, he appeared first to Mary Magdalene, out of whom he had driven seven demons. She went and told those who had been with him and who were mourning and weeping. When they heard that Jesus was alive and that she had seen him, they did not believe it. Afterward Jesus appeared in a different form to two of them while they were walking in the country. These returned and reported it to the rest; but they did not believe them either. Later Jesus appeared to the Eleven as they were eating; he rebuked them for their lack of faith and their stubborn refusal to believe those who had seen him after he had risen."

Matthew 5:16 (p. 26) – "Let your light so shine..."

Matthew 6:4 (p. 62) – "...so that your giving may be in secret. Then your Father, who sees what is done in secret, will reward you."

Matthew 6:5-6 (p. 62) –
"And when you pray, do not be like the hypocrites, for they love to pray standing in the synagogues and on the street corners to be seen by others. Truly I tell you, they have received their reward in full. But when you pray, go into your room, close the door and pray to your Father, who is unseen. Then your Father, who sees what is done in secret, will reward you."

Matthew 6:19-20 (p. 34) –
"Do not store up for yourselves treasures on earth, where moths and vermin destroy, and where thieves break in and steal.

But store up for yourselves treasures in heaven, where moths and vermin do not destroy, and where thieves do not break in and steal."

Matthew 12:50 (p. 48) –
"For whoever does the will of my Father in heaven is my brother and sister and mother."

Matthew 18:4 (p. 30) – "Therefore, whoever takes the lowly position of this child is the greatest in the kingdom of heaven."

Matthew 25:40 (p. 12, p. 66) – "The King will reply, 'Truly I tell you, whatever you did for one of the least of these brothers and sisters of mine, you did for me.'"

2 Peter 1:5, 7 (p. 12) – "For this very reason, make every effort to add to your faith goodness; and to goodness, knowledge... and to godliness, mutual affection; and to mutual affection, love."

Proverbs 13:3 (p. 38) – "Those who guard their lips preserve their lives, but those who speak rashly will come to ruin."

Psalm 32:6 (p. 64) – "Therefore let all the faithful pray to you while you may be found; surely the rising of the mighty waters will not reach them."

Psalm 33:4 (p. 28) – "For the word of the Lord is right and true; he is faithful in all he does."

Psalm 46:10 (p. 24) – "He says, 'Be still, and know that I am God; I will be exalted among the nations, I will be exalted in the earth.'"

Psalm 139:13-16 (p. 42) – "For you created my inmost being; you knit me together in my mother's womb. I praise you because I am fearfully and wonderfully made; your works are wonderful, I know that full well. My frame was not hidden from you when I was made in the secret place, when I was woven together in the depths of the earth. Your eyes saw my unformed body; all the days ordained for me were written in your book before one of them came to be."

Psalm 139:14 (p. 43) – "I praise you because I am fearfully and wonderfully made; your works are wonderful, I know that full well."

Psalm 143:9 (p. 8) – "Rescue me from my enemies, Lord, for I hide myself in you."

Psalm 147:3 (p. 44) – "He heals the brokenhearted and binds up their wounds."

Romans 12:2 (p. 72) – "Do not conform to the pattern of this world, but be transformed by the renewing of your mind. Then you will be able to test and approve what God's will is—his good, pleasing and perfect will."

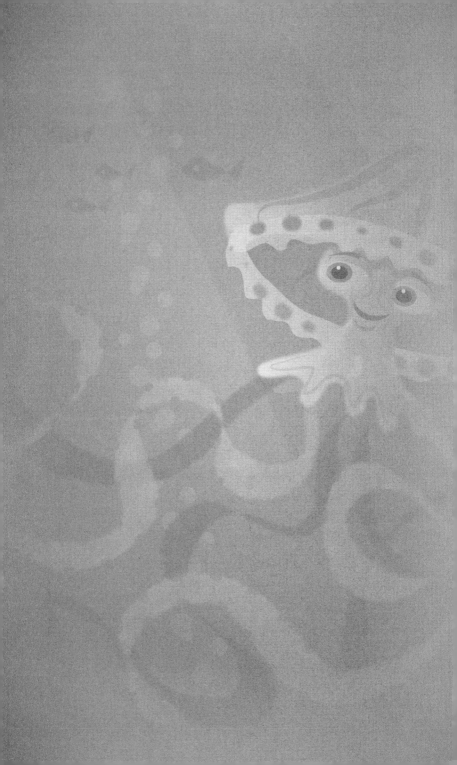